Printed in Canada.

ISBN 0-15-359601-5

ISBN 978-0-15-359601-8

11 1774 16 15 14 13 12

4500343077

Harcourt
SCHOOL PUBLISHERS
www.harcourtschool.com

CONTENTS

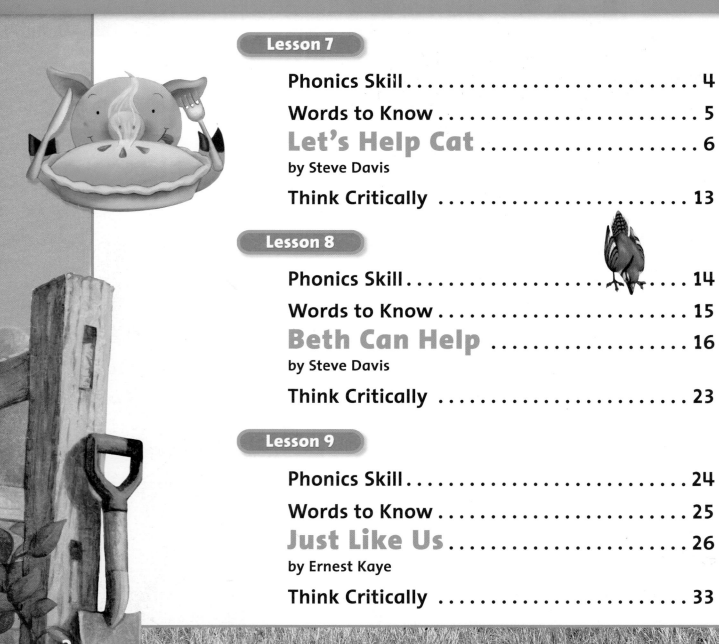

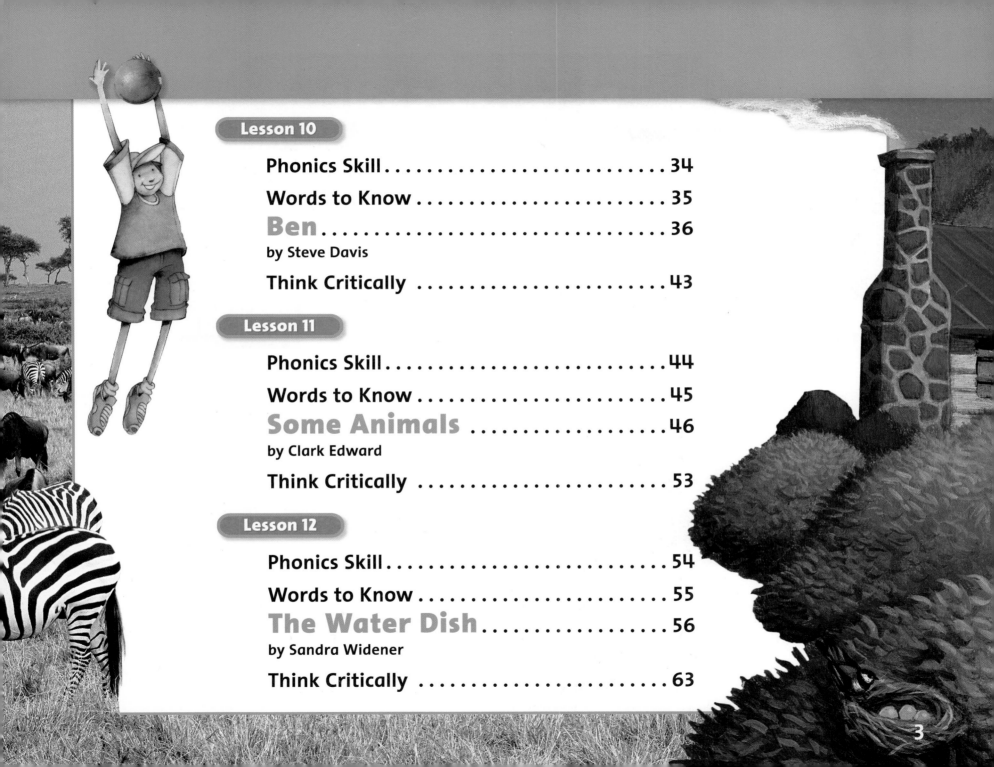

Phonics Skill

Read each word. Circle the word that names each picture.

1.

2.

3.

4. tell ten

5. tell hen

6. hen tell

4

Words to Know

make

said

eat

Read the words. Then read each sentence. Trace the word that completes the sentence.

1. "That looks good," ___said___ Pig.

2. "Let's ___make___ it," said Cat.

3. "Now we will ___eat___ it!" said Pig.

Let's Help Cat

by Steve Davis

illustrations by Claudine Ge'Vry

"Let's make a pie," said Cat.

"Yes!" said Hen.

"I will mix it," said Goat.

"I will help," said Horse.

"I will get a pan," said Cow.

"I will eat it!" said Pig.

"We will eat it!" said Cat.

Think Critically

Circle the best answer.

I. What did the friends make?

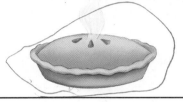  

2. What happened first?

3. How does Cow help?

WRITE What do you like to make? Write or draw about it on a separate sheet of paper.

©Harcourt

Phonics Skill

Read each word. Circle the word that names each picture.

1.

2.

3.

4. bath thick

5. thick thin

6. bath thin

©Harcourt

14

Words to Know

says

water

her

Read the words. Then read each sentence. Trace the word that completes the sentence.

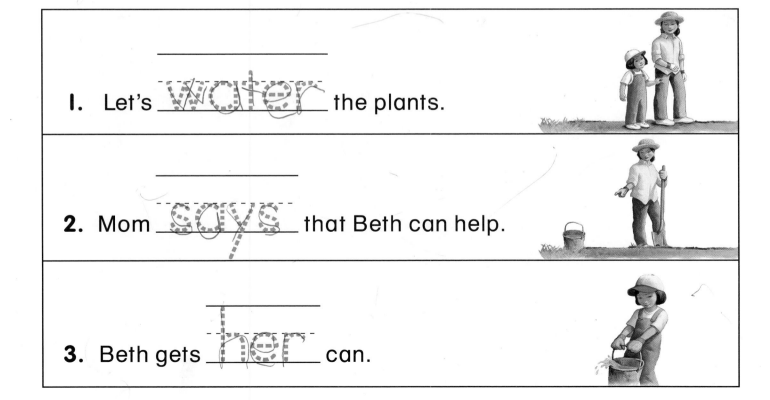

1. Let's _____ water _____ the plants.

2. Mom _____ says _____ that Beth can help.

3. Beth gets _____ her _____ can.

Beth Can Help

by Steve Davis

illustrations by Steve Johnson and Lou Fancher

Mom says that Beth can dig.

"Get a shovel, Beth."

Mom says that Beth can plant.

"Get some seeds, Beth."

Mom says that Beth can water.

"Get a bucket, Beth."

Look! Her plants got big!

Think Critically

Circle the best answer.

1. Where does the story take place?

2. Who gives Beth seeds?

3. How does the story end?

WRITE How would you help in the garden? Write or draw about it on a separate sheet of paper.

Phonics Skill

Read each word. Circle the word that names each picture.

1.  u p

2. n u t

3.  t r u c k

4.  (nut)   truck

5.  (up)   truck

6.  up   (truck)

Words to Know

grow

food

live

Read the words. Then read each sentence. Trace the word that completes the sentence.

1. They _____live_____ here, just like us.

2. They can _____grow_____ up, just like us.

3. They eat _____food_____, just like us.

Just Like Us

by Ernest Kaye

illustrations by Jeff Crosby

Look at the trees.

They grow up, just like us.

Look at the birds.

They must get water, just like us.

Look at the deer.

They eat food, just like us.

They live here, just like us!

Think Critically

Circle the best answer.

1. What do the people look at first?

2. What are the birds getting?

3. Where do they all live?

WRITE What plants or animals live near you? Write or draw about them on a separate sheet of paper.

Phonics Skill

Read each word. Circle the word that names each picture.

1.

2.

3.

4.  strong (swing)

5.  (strong) ring

6.  swing (ring)

Words to Know

school

your

arms

Read the words. Then read each sentence. Trace the word that completes the sentence.

1. Bring _____your_____ ball, Ben!

2. Ben holds the ball in his _____arms_____ .

3. Let's go to _____school_____ now.

©Harcourt

35

Ben

by Steve Davis

illustrations by Benoit Laverdiere

The boys see Ben at school.

"Bring your ball, Ben."

The boys see Ben kick the ball.

"Your legs are so strong, Ben!"

The boys see Ben get the ball.

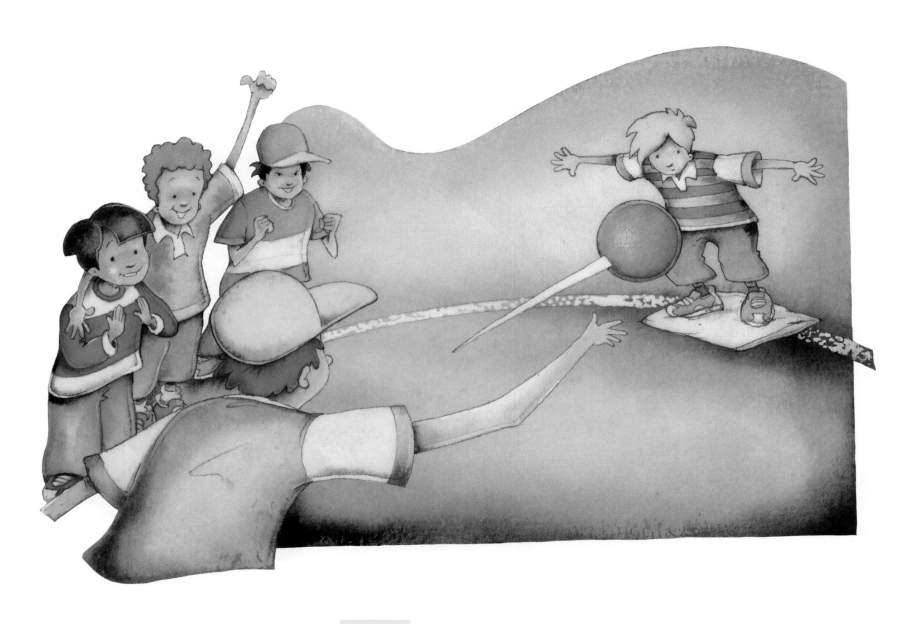

"Your arms are so long, Ben!"

Ben will help us win!

Think Critically

Circle the best answer.

1. Where does the story take place?

  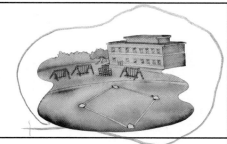

2. What does Ben have?

3. How does the story end?

WRITE What sport do you like to play? Write or draw about it on a separate sheet of paper.

Phonics Skill

Read each word. Circle the word that names each picture.

1.

2.

3.

4.  fork   corn

5. corn   store

6. fork   store

Words to Know

cold

animals

from

Read the words. Then read each sentence. Trace the word that completes the sentence.

1. Some ___animals___ live where it is wet.

2. This animal is ___from___ a hot land.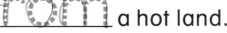

3. This animal lives in a ___cold___ land.

Some Animals

by Clark Edward

Some animals are from a cold land.

This penguin wants more food.

Some animals are from a hot land.

This camel stores water in its hump.

Some animals are from a wet land.

This seal looks for a snack.

All animals like to eat!

Think Critically

Circle the best answer.

1. Which animal is from a cold land?

2. What would a penguin eat?

3. Where are camels from?

WRITE Which place would you like to visit? Write or draw
about it on a separate sheet of paper.

Phonics Skill

Read each word. Circle the word that names each picture.

1. b r u s h

2. d i s h

3. s h e l l

4. dish   shell

5. shell   dish

6. brush   dish

©Harcourt

Words to Know

saw

could

was

Read the words. Then read each sentence. Trace the word that completes the sentence.

1. She  saw water in a dish.

2. The dish  was too tall.

3. She could not get a drink.

©Harcourt

55

The Water Dish

by Sandra Widener

illustrations by Juliet Howard

Bird wanted a drink.

She saw water in a dish.

Bird **could** not get a drink.

What could she do?

Splash! She could drop shells in!

Now she could get a drink.

The water was good!

Think Critically

Circle the best answer.

1. Where does the story take place?

  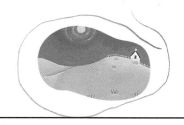

2. What does Bird drop into the dish?

3. How did Bird solve her problem?

WRITE What is a problem you had to solve? Write or draw about it on a separate sheet of paper.